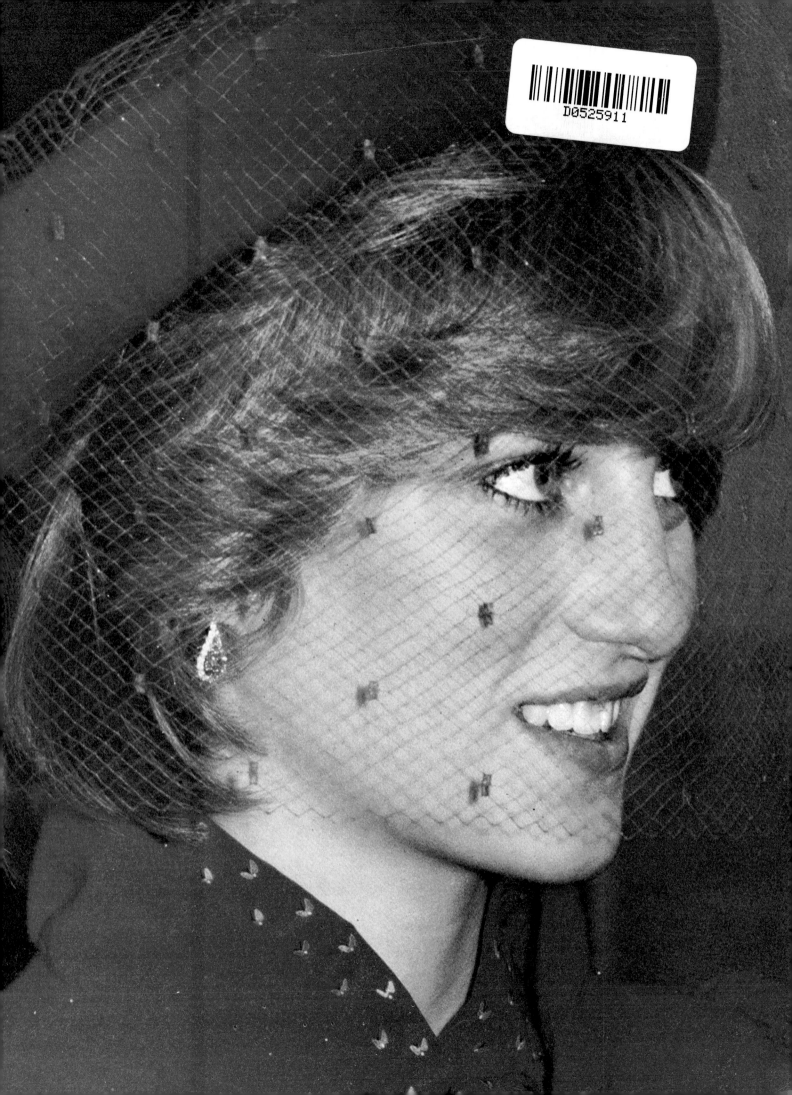

GOD BLESS THE PRINCESS OF WALES

TEXT BY CHRISTOPHER BENTHAM-SMITH

CORGI BOOKS

A DIVISION OF
TRANSWORLD PUBLISHERS LTD

INTRODUCTION

Unlike the vast majority of Britain's nine Princesses of Wales, the birth of Lady Diana Frances Spencer was nationally and internationally unheralded and unsung. Her personal circumstances have been the subject of public interest on only two major occasions: once briefly but unpleasantly in 1969 when her parents were divorced and contested a highly publicised court case over custody of their children; and again, more extensively and much more agreeably when rumours of her growing attachment to Charles Prince of Wales began to spread and gain credence.

On the day following the official announcement of her engagement, the Press were ready with an immensity of detail about Lady Diana's background. This was understandable enough since it is not every day that the heir apparent to the Throne becomes engaged —indeed the last time this happened was almost 120 years before, when the future King Edward VII was betrothed to Princess Alexandra, the eldest daughter of Prince Christian (later King Christian IX) of Denmark. But the intense public fascination with Lady Diana's background stemmed from the

Above *Once a Lady, now a Princess. Diana at Broadlands in May 1981.*
Opposite *Lord Snowdon's majestic official portrait of Diana, taken at Highgrove soon after her engagement.*

to carry on the Spencer name and lineage. And a boy it was —named John after his father, and born to extend the Earldom of Spencer into the seventh generation. But by the twist of fate that has also deprived the firstborn sons of British sovereigns of the succession, baby John's inheritance was not to last. He died later on the day of his birth, and the Althorps, though parents of two daughters, were still without a male heir. Haunted by the memory of that confinement it was with some trepidation that they looked forward to this next birth. As it happened, it was an easy one and it produced yet another daughter. If the parents were disappointed it was not for long: the baby was a good healthy specimen weighing almost eight pounds, and it survived.

It is almost perversely ironic that in contrast with so many of her predecessors as Princess of Wales who came from palaces all over Europe to marry into the British royal house, this non-royal baby should have been born within half a mile of Sandringham— the favourite country residence, next to Windsor, of the present Royal Family. Diana

knowledge and admiration of the fact that from a life of very private activities, this 19-year-old girl was being catapulted into a rôle which was to prepare her for the undreamed-of and unenviable task of being Britain's next Queen Consort.

The prospect was indeed a far cry from the June days in 1961 when the then Viscount and Viscountess Althorp looked forward to the birth of the baby who, in events, would fill that position. The auspices were not good. Only eighteen months before, the parents had been awaiting with excited anticipation the birth of their third child, and hoping that it would be a boy,

was born at Park House, one of several substantial houses on the Sandringham estate which successive sovereigns have over the years tenanted to family friends and retainers. This rambling old house, built like Sandringham itself in the mid-nineteenth century, was originally leased to the Fermoy family by King George V through his great friend Edmund, 4th Baron Fermoy. Unlike many grace and favour homes, the lease was continued after the old King's death and Lord Fermoy, with his wife Ruth, enjoyed their occupation of it until his own death in 1955. It was then leased by the present Queen to Viscount Althorp as a

token of the great friendship which the Spencers had established with the Royal Family over the years.

The Spencer family has long been associated with British sovereigns. It stems from the great Duke of Marlborough, for whom Queen Anne ordered the building of Blenheim Palace in the early years of the eighteenth century. His grandson John Spencer inherited much of the Marlborough wealth through the Duke's widow Sarah, and became Ranger of Windsor Great Park. His son—like many successors to the title, he was also named John—was raised to the peerage as the first Earl Spencer, and it was his children who began in earnest the pattern of aristocratic inter-marriage which has, to those for whom these things carry significance. helped to give Lady Diana's antecedents a rare brilliance. His daughers' marriages connected him with the wealthy Earls of Bessborough and the prestigious Dukes of Devonshire, while his son and heir George married Lavinia, daughter of the first Earl of Lucan—the head of a family which was to achieve notoriety in the Crimea and indeed in the twentieth century. George Spencer also became First Lord of the Admiralty; his elder son John, the 3rd Earl, was Chancellor of the Exchequer in Queen Victoria's reign, and the younger son Frederick, who eventually became the fourth Earl, served in the Queen's household. Frederick married twice—by his first wife he had a son John who inherited as the fifth Earl, and who became Groom of the Stole to King Edward VII as Prince of Wales, as well as holding three major ministerial posts in government. Frederick's second wife—a daughter of the Marquess of Hertford—bore him two children: a daughter for whom Queen Victoria acted as godmother and who was appropriately named Victoria Alexandrina; and a son Charles who was Groom in Waiting to Queen Victoria and Lord Chamberlain in the households of King Edward VII and King George V. Charles became the sixth Earl Spencer: Queen Alexandra was godmother to one of his daughters, while two other daughters became members of the household of Queen Elizabeth the Queen Mother. Of Charles' three sons, one had children to whom Prince George Duke of Kent and Queen Maud of Norway were godparents. The eldest of Charles' sons, Albert Edward John—later the seventh Earl—married one of the present Queen Mother's Ladies of the Bedchamber and this couple became the parents of the present (eighth) Lord Spencer.

It is to the seventh Earl that the impressive collection of objets d'art and pictures at the family seat at Althorp in Northamptonshire is largely due—he spent his life consolidating and extending the mighty array of family heirlooms which now form part of the Spencer inheritance, in the same way as his royal contemporary Queen Mary avidly collected throughout her long life. Thus in 1975, on the death of the seventh Earl, Viscount Althorp inherited a colossal family fortune as well as the awesome economic burden of maintaining a huge stately home in an age when the financial liability of preserving any large undertaking in its unspoilt entirety has defeated many a landed aristocrat.

Last glance back for the new Princess: even the police turn their heads and Diana looks up the Mall as she and Charles ride past Carlton House Terrace on their way from Buckingham Palace to Waterloo Station to begin their honeymoon.

Prince Andrew's contribution to this colourful picture is seen in the helium-filled blue and silver balloons and "Just Married" notice which he and Prince Edward had attached to the carriage.

This potted family history shows that Lady Diana's ancestry is a colourful and distinguished one. It has the added lustre of direct royal connections in that she is, through various female branches, descended five times from Charles II though only by virtue, if that is the right word, of his liaisons with mistresses. Further descents from Henry VII have also been traced.

The character of Lady Diana's life at home, which was obviously very secure financially, was unsullied by any materialistic influence of the considerable family fortune. Her father was, until 1975, only the heir to it and not its possessor, and he contented himself with an existence based on farming in Norfolk, his interest in cricket and his support for local charities and good causes. Diana, with her two elder sisters—Sarah, born in 1955, and Jane, born in 1957—ran almost a menagerie of domestic pets which included horses, ponies, dogs and rabbits, and smaller cage animals such as hamsters and guinea-pigs. She liked horses in particular, and maintained that love even after a fall from her pony when she was ten discouraged her from persisting with riding as a hobby.

Everything revolved around home, and they were palmy days. Like the children of many aristocractic families, even in this age of relentless democratisation, Diana and her sisters were educated at home—by an indulgent teacher Miss Gertrude Allen, who, sadly, died before her former charge married the heir to the Throne. With her schooling, her hobbies and her family life in general centred around the crisp scenery of this placidly rural part of Norfolk, Diana enjoyed little contact with the outside world—nor did she need to. The family was complete when in 1964 her mother gave birth to the long awaited male child who is now Charles, Viscount Althorp.

Regrettably this seemingly happy state of affairs did not endure. In 1967, with an abruptness which startled and baffled not only her husband but also the entire household and their circle of friends, Diana's mother left Park House—to join, it was learned in due course, Mr Peter Shand Kydd whom she married less than three years later. The family structure at Park House immediately fell to pieces. Diana's home teacher was dismissed, Sarah and Jane were packed off to school in King's Lynn and Diana, temporarily in the care of her maternal grandmother Ruth, Lady Fermoy, and subsequently looked after by a succession of *au pair* girls, was eventually sent to a boarding school, Riddlesworth Hall, near Diss. Her head teacher, Miss Ridsdale, who is still alive, noticed that despite Diana's very particular conduct—she was obedient, methodical, hardworking and punctilious—her educational progress was slow. By nature quiet and unobtrusive, she suffered, as she was to at a later date, from homesickness, and not unnaturally simply failed to settle into her new school life for some time.

Even when she became more familiar with her new surroundings her academic development, though just adequate, was unspectacular and certainly fell far short of the more sporting achievements which led her, amongst other things, to represent her school in swimming competitions. At the age of twelve she moved to West Heath School in Kent, but by that time her home life was losing its original identity: she was spending her holidays alternately with her mother at the Shand Kydd farm in Western Scotland—a perfect springboard for visits to the Western Isles—and with her father at Park House.

Further fundamental changes quickly followed. In 1975, when the 7th Earl Spencer died and Diana's father inherited the

Earldom, he gave up his tenancy of his home of twenty years for the architectural and cultural splendour of Althorp's fifteen thousand acres in the heart of Northamptonshire's gently contoured countryside. The next year Lord Spencer remarried, and this brought another shift of domestic emphasis. Diana's new stepmother was the former Lady Dartmouth, the elegant socialite Raine, daughter of the novelist Barbara Cartland. The new Countess of Spencer lost no time in establishing herself as mistress of Althorp and rationalising changes in policy and administration began forthwith.

By this time, Diana's two elder sisters had attained their majorities and began to carve out their own personal lives. Diana was at that time still at school, which she decided to leave soon after her sixteenth birthday. She was then sent to a finishing school in Switzerland, the exclusive Institut Alpin Videmanette, a fashionable establishment in an exclusive part of Rougement,

where she learned domestic skills and French. It was odd that, despite the instability of her life in England, she failed to outstay the course in Switzerland, and that she was back only six months after she first joined it suffering from acute homesickness, and feeling that further academic or social training was not for her.

Soon after her return, her father bought her a large flat at Coleherne Court in the Old Brompton Road in Knightsbridge, and Diana began the free and easy life of a bachelor girl in the

Diana's love of children has been her hallmark, and no walkabout is complete without at least a few minutes devoted to them as in Builth Wells (1, 2) in October 1981. It was an early characteristic: (3) Diana is photographed in September 1980 with two children from the kindergarten where she worked.

company of three flatmates: Carolyn Pride, Anne Bolton and Virginia Pitman. Their loyal and discreet treatment of the news which she would one day confide to them was to be of major personal significance and value to her. Meanwhile, Diana looked around for a regular occupation, and eventually found it as an assistant teacher at the Young England Kindergarten School in Pimlico, run by Miss Kay Seth-Smith. And it was here that, in the daily company of young and dependent children, she might have formed the basis of a lifelong vocation.

But the Spencer family's long association with the House of Windsor directed otherwise. Diana knew the family well, of course. In her teens she had been great friends with Prince Andrew and Prince Edward, who often came over from Sandringham House to swim in the Spencers' pool which had been installed in the late sixties. Later she had joined Prince Charles on pheasant shoots at Sandringham, but these were casual, almost routine, meetings with no deeper significance than that of strong friendship. By 1978 Diana's sister Jane had married—to one of the Queen's assistant private secretaries—and in the same year her other sister Sarah had joined Prince

Diana samples her first taste of publicity in September 1980 as she leaves the Young England Kindergarten in Pimlico at the end of the school day. Scenes like these occurred almost daily as the world's press became increasingly aware of

the free facilities for photographing the latest prospect for the position of Princess of Wales, and by November Diana was almost being chased through the streets in her efforts to avoid them.

and ski-ing holidays in Switzerland. In August 1979, Diana was enjoying a Bank Holiday picnic at Balmoral with the Prince and other members of his family when at midday came the appalling news of Lord Mountbatten's murder at Mullaghmore. It is said that Prince Charles' inconsolable grief and Diana's natural solicitous concern for him brought them very close together on

this regrettably momentous occasion. There is little doubt that it must have contributed to their closeness because the following year Diana was at Balmoral again—ostensibly to assist her sister Jane with the birth of her first child. At the beginning of August Prince Charles arrived and events began to move with some speed. Although Diana was due to leave for London shortly afterwards, further meetings between her and the Prince were arranged, mostly in a way which would avoid raising the suspicions of the Press who were ever on the scent for the next stage in the Prince's long and hitherto unaccomplished search for a wife. One such carefully planned meeting involved an invitation to Diana to stay with the Queen Mother at Birkhall, her Highland home close to Balmoral. Nevertheless it was not long before the news leaked out. One day in September a

Charles on his annual ski-ing holiday at Klosters in Switzerland. For a time the Press saw Lady Sarah as the firm favourite for the choice of a royal bride, but shortly after the holiday Sarah talked unintentionally openly about her friendship with the Prince, and like at least one other of his many girlfriends she forfeited his close attentions: public declarations about private matters of this sort are anathema to the Palace and no-one has yet been known to have survived the breach of this rule.

But Lady Diana—then only sixteen—had not gone unnoticed in the course of Prince Charles' close acquaintance with her sister. The Prince got to know and be seen with several girls since those early months of 1978 but Diana kept cropping up as one who shared his company on occasions less public than the usual polo matches at Windsor, race meetings at Royal Ascot

photographer spotted Charles and Diana fishing together in the River Dee and within a few days the whole Press had been alerted and were tracking her down to her flat where she had recently returned ready for the new school term. Her life in the alluring but relentless glare of international publicity had begun.

For Diana, with her essentially private personality and her background of withdrawal from contention and conspicuity, that publicity was totally unsought and unwanted. From what we can now glean of her character it is unlikely that she failed to appreciate the interest that her romance with Charles would involve, though whether she could have imagined its intensity or persistence is another matter. She found, much to her despair, that there was no question of public curiosity being sated after the first few days—on the contrary the more she was inevitably obliged to appear in public, even for the few minutes it took her to dash from her flat to her car, and from her car to the kindergarten building, the more the world's army of photographers and reporters crowded in on her. The clicking and whirring of the cameras were the continuous accompaniment to her daily round. Reporters dogged her footsteps and peppered her with questions as she strode—sometimes with her head held high, sometimes with her hands covering her face—through the lines of curious onlookers.

For sheer self-assurance, she was unbeatable. She dealt with all questions with as much patience as time would allow, but rarely gave more away than the obvious fact that she was not prepared to comment. To the specific question: "Has Prince Charles proposed to you?" she answered candidly but almost teasingly: "I really can't answer questions like that." But even this comparatively open approach to the commercial interest of her questioners failed to discourage them, and at length things became so bad that her mother wrote a letter to The Times to complain of harassment. The letter forced Fleet Street to consider the issues involved, but the probing went on. A great furore arose the following January when the Royal Family's annual New Year pheasant-shooting holiday at Sandringham gave photographers and reporters the opportunity to scan the estate for signs of Diana's presence. Prince Charles attempted to put them off with feigned surprise: "I can't imagine what you are all here for." Then he used a rather tantalising form of cajolerie: "You will all know in good time." Finally, his patience broke and in a now memorable phrase he wished "you all a Happy New Year and your editors a particularly nasty one."

Diana was at Sandringham for a few days during that holiday but the Press saw little if anything of her. Little did they know either that Prince Charles had already proposed to her and that she had been inclined to accept. He, however, had insisted that she should give the matter further thought, and that she should take the opportunity of a holiday in Australia, which had been arranged some time before, to consider. Only a few days after her departure, she was on the telephone to him to say that she would marry him. Prince Charles then contacted Lord Spencer for permission to marry his daughter and Lord Spencer was delighted to say yes—though he mischievously wondered afterwards what would have happened had he refused!

Diana enjoyed the remainder of her Australian holiday in comparative peace before returning to Britain. Although her arrival back at Heathrow Airport was reported, it was treated with an absence of sensation which suggested either that the public had lost interest in the supposed romance, or that there was no news value left in the story. As it happened, however, the Queen and the whole of her family had been informed of the Prince's decision, and a huge dinner party was given at Windsor on the weekend of 21st/22nd February to celebrate it. The occasion was tinged with sadness because on the previous Friday Prince Charles' promising steeplechaser Allibar dropped

Engaged at last: a happy Lady Diana leans on her fiancé as they pose for photographs at Buckingham Palace just four hours after their engagement had been announced. On the fourth finger of Diana's left hand is the £28,000 sapphire and diamond engagement ring which *Charles had bought her. Opposite A royal cuddle for Lord Snowdon's official photograph, released for publication on a special issue of stamps: one of the most informal engagement photographs of a royal couple ever published.*

dead as he was being walked back from a training session at Lambourne. The Press had not been slow to pick up the significance of the fact that Diana was present on that occasion to console the Prince who was badly upset by the death of his horse. By Tuesday 24th February, however, the speculation which was on the point of being revived, was itself put down by the official announcement from Buckingham Palace at 11 o'clock that "It is with the greatest pleasure that the Queen and the Duke of Edinburgh announce the betrothal of their beloved son the Prince of Wales to the Lady Diana Spencer . . ."

There was no mistaking Diana's relief once the news was public. Four hours after the announcement she and her fiancé

In May 1981, Diana accompanied Charles to Broadlands, formerly the home of Lord Mountbatten, where Charles opened the four-month exhibition of Mountbatten memorabilia. The opening was the only formal part of the day: afterwards the couple went into the grounds of the 6,000-acre estate to plant a commemorative tree. Diana took the opportunity to meet some of the hundreds of spectators who came to see them. (1) A low level conference between Diana and a bemused toddler; (2) Diana's confidence to Charles at the tree-planting ceremony; (3, 4) Diana enjoying her walkabout.

1

2

3

were out on the spacious lawns at the front of Buckingham Palace posing for photographers whose pictures would tell their own happy story. She walked hand in hand with Prince Charles, beaming with contentment, exchanged pleasantries with the photographers and showed off her beautiful sapphire and diamond ring for which Prince Charles had just paid some £28,000. Everyone seemed delighted with the news: the official announcement told of the Queen's great pleasure; Lord Spencer and his former wife were reunited in the sheer joy of seeing their youngest daughter engaged in a true love-match with the man who one day would be King; Barbara Cartland, the mother of the new Countess Spencer, rhapsodised over the idyll of aristocratic young love which was taking place before the eyes of the

4

Opposite *Diana with her posy of lilies, iris and roses, during the Broadlands walkabout. Overleaf stunning studies in red: (1) Diana at the Guildford Cathedral Christmas celebration in aid of the Prince's Trust in December 1981; (2) another engagement portrait by Snowdon, showing Diana wearing a blouse with the sort of ruffle with which she has become exclusively identified.*

1

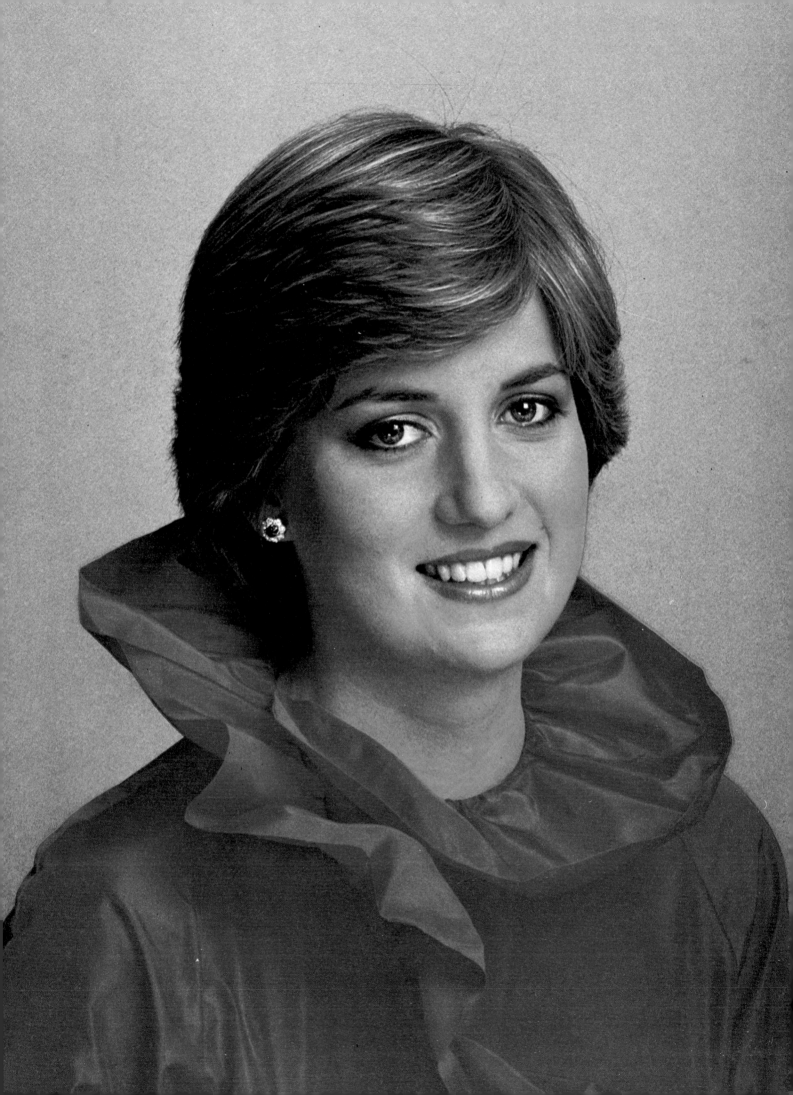

How things have changed. (1, 2)
Diana is tight-lipped when leaving her flat in Knightsbridge to travel to the kindergarten in November 1980, just after the weekend she spent at Sandringham with Charles to

celebrate his thirty-third birthday; (3) openly gratified by the flowers heaped upon her by the children of Cardiff after she had received the Freedom of the City at the end of October 1981.

nation; the thousands of people gathered against the railings of the Palace as the news began to spread shouted and sang and speculated with an intensity rarely witnessed, and the national and provincial press made the inevitable and effusive contribution in columns of words and pictures illustrating the lives and antecedents of the couple and comparing the forthcoming marriage with those of previous Princes of Wales. It was over a month later, more officially, the Privy Council gave its constitutional consent to the marriage, following which Diana was for the first time officially photographed with the Queen.

The wedding which would make Diana the first Princess of Wales for over seventy years was fixed for the 29th July—only five months later, and within a month of her own 20th birthday. Five months was a long time by royal standards, but the circumstances were rather special. Not only did substantial preparations have to be made for what was already being billed as "The Wedding of the Century" but Diana herself, a complete stranger to the formal and official side of royal existence, had to be introduced to as many facets of the life-style of a member of the Royal Family as possible. She had refused to admit, when she was first interviewed after the engagement, that she had ever had any doubts about her decision to marry, and many people secretly wondered whether this wasn't a rather immature and ingenuous attitude by a mere 19-year-old to the awesome responsibilities of a prospective Princess of Wales. We now know that in fact she has a mind very much of her own, and the

will to tackle almost anything with supreme confidence. That confidence manifested itself on the very first public engagement which she undertook with Prince Charles—an evening recital in the City of London—when she wore a spectacularly low-cut evening dress in black taffeta, quite the most daring creation anyone could have expected of her. And she walked between the two huge batteries of photographers' flash-lights without so much as a blush!

It was as much as anything a gesture of self-assurance, and it made people admire her greatly. It proclaimed itself on many a subsequent occasion during which Diana established her very own style, consisting most noticeably of a new approachability—a disposition to spend time talking with people she met, to walk among crowds without necessarily always keeping the royal distance, to repay the attentions people gave her with her own presence and interest. On her various visits out of London—most of these were to towns in the West Country like Cheltenham, Cirencester and Tetbury—she was soon to become famous for her spontaneous gestures of goodwill. In a now celebrated incident she allowed a schoolboy the gallant liberty of kissing

Making friends with children; Diana looking very much at home with babies and youngsters on her various outings. (1) At Broadlands in May 1981, she picks up and cuddles a baby from the crowd; (2) taking flowers from a reluctant admirer in Hyde Park in November 1981 after she and Charles had planted trees to commemorate their wedding and their own forthcoming baby; (3) Diana with a group of children in South Wales in October 1981; (4) Who's that down there? Diana seems too surprised for words as shyness overwhelms one Welsh child.

her hand as his "future Queen"; in another she took over a babe in arms and cradled it while chatting to its mother; in yet another she repaid one little boy';s persistence by pulling his cap over his eyes. Much of her time on walkabouts was spent crouching down in conversation with toddlers with some tale to tell or flowers to offer. It was soon appreciated, with universal approval, that her speciality, like her calling, seemed to be to children, and the performance of her official duties with this emphatic new interpretation added a new dimension to the manner in which royalty was expected to behave.

At the same time Diana was schooled in the more formal requirements of occasions of state. By the time of her wedding she had been present at three State banquets, the Service of the Order of the Garter, the Trooping the Colour ceremony, the presentation of colours at Windsor. In that time she also made her début at several events which now form the modern London season, attending the four days of Royal Ascot, several days of polo at Windsor and elsewhere, and odd days watching the tennis championships at Wimbledon. She allowed herself two spells of comparative isolation from the public—one during the

Diana's preference in clothes has sometimes bordered on the theatrical, but they always seemed to match the occasion in 1981. (1) A shimmering, filmy, off-the-shoulder evening dress to suit the "Splendours of the Gonzaga" exhibition at the Victoria and Albert Museum in November. (2) Ruffled collars and sleeves for a light grey gown at Claridge's where she attended the King of Saudi-Arabia's State Banquet in June. (3) A breezy informal dress for switching on the Regent Street Christmas lights in December. (4) A low-cut blue evening dress for a soirée at the Royal Academy of Arts in June. (5) Emerald green taffeta, jewels and a black cape for a cold night in Swansea in October.

five-week tour which Prince Charles made in Australia and New Zealand in April and May, and again during the three weeks before the wedding itself, when her nerves were beginning to feel the strain. It was almost on the eve of the wedding that her otherwise impenetrable composure began to falter. On the Saturday prior to the great day she accompanied Prince Charles to Windsor to watch him play polo. The Queen, several members of the Royal Family, and many distinguished guests who

had already arrived to attend the wedding, were there. Understandably enough, the Press, there in full force for the last public appearance of Diana as a single woman—had eyes only for her. Their enthusiasm for pictures outstripped their consideration for her comfort or freedom of movement, and they followed her every step as she vainly attempted to enjoy the afternoon's events. Ultimately it all proved too much and, almost without warning, she made a dash for her car where the consoling arm of her companion Lady Romsey made it obvious to everyone that Diana was in tears. It was a dramatic and unhappy end to what had been a highly successful apprenticeship for the job she was about to take on, and it was with some inkling of remorse that the Press realised that they had, on that last occasion, gone too far.

Happily, as Prince Charles revealed the following morning, no lasting harm had been done, and all attentions were turned to the approaching wedding day. Diana had attended several rehearsals at St Paul's Cathedral, and as London began to fill up with people and traffic, there was a general confidence, encouraged partly by the superb weather, that everything was going to go well. With five months of intense and meticulous preparation now completed, it was hardly conceivable that,

Diana, bright with anticipation, during her visit to South Wales at the end of October 1981; her jaunty Belleville-Sassoon hat and frilled collar gave her a swashbuckling appearance. Opposite *Plain and pensive: A hatless Diana in tartan plaid during the tree-planting ceremony in Hyde Park in November 1981.*

barring divine interference, anything could possibly go wrong.

And so it proved on the day. Lady Diana, on her last day as such, was awakened at Clarence House shortly after dawn. Her attendants—hairdressers, make-up artist, dressmakers—were all ready to begin the long, perfectionist task of preparing her for the principal part in the pure theatre which was to follow. Outside, the crowds were also awake early, watching eagerly as police and troops marched up and down to take up their positions along the two miles of processional route. From just before ten o'clock, contingent after contingent of royal and distinguished guests began to leave Buckingham Palace in shining limousines *en route* for St Paul's. Their successive appearance heightened the excitement of the crowds pressed thickly around the Queen Victoria Memorial and along the pavements running down the Mall.

One of the most popular spots, taken up and filled earlier than any other, was the area surrounding the approach road

linking the Mall with Clarence House, where the bride would make her first appearance in that hitherto secret wedding dress. And shortly after the last of the eight royal carriages had left the Palace—the very last of all carrying Prince Charles himself—all eyes and hundreds of cameras were turned upon Clarence House.

When at last Diana appeared, there was a sensation. Riding in the dainty and compact Glass Coach—the transport of royal brides for nearly sixty years—she sat, next to her proud father, ensconced in a mass of lace and tulle which gave every indication that the dress would be a magnificently romantic creation. Already the crowds could see her glittering tiara—an heirloom from the Spencer vaults—which, apart from a pair of drop

3

ear-rings, was the only piece of jewellery she wore. Of course she was acclaimed on all sides during her twenty-minute drive to the Cathedral. The sheer happiness of the occasion, the sense of being present at a greatly historic moment, the colour and spectacle provided by flags, bunting, decorations, flowers, red-coated soldiers, beautifully groomed horses and the gleaming, lacquered carriages made the crowds ecstatic, and their heroine responded blushingly from behind her ivory veil.

What was to come was probably the greatest test of Diana's nerves. Hitherto completely self-confident, would she stand up to the demands of a ceremony the like of which had not been seen for generations? In the event she managed it all with consummate ease. She bore an additional responsibility in that her father, still showing the signs of the severe brain haemorrhage which had almost killed him three years earlier, had had to be assisted up the Cathedral steps and was so unsteady on his feet that it was Diana who had to support *him* as she made her way up the aisle, rather than *vice versa*. He later testified gratefully to her confidence: "She was a tower of strength to me," he said. And as the marriage service began its sonorous, almost melodramatic course, Diana with her self-assured presence and —barring the now famous fluffed line when she repeated Prince Charles' four names in the wrong order—firm and un-equivocal replies, contributed to the smooth, joyful and meaningful ceremonial of the occasion. Each of her vows, as well as

4

Wedding day for Diana, and Lord Lichfield's formal portrait puts the happy occasion into historical perspective. (1) Charles, in his uniform of a naval Commander, stands with Diana in the Throne Room of Buckingham Palace. (2) Diana alone, posed to show her magnificent ivory tulle train and waterfall bouquet of half-a-dozen different flowers. (3) A close-up of Diana in her sequined dress, trimmed with lace and studded with mother of pearl. She wears the Spencer tiara. (4) Diana enters St Paul's Cathedral on the arm of her father, Lord Spencer, and is followed by bridesmaids Lady Sarah Armstrong-Jones and India Hicks.

those of Prince Charles and the pronouncements of the Archbishop of Canterbury, was greeted by a huge wave of cheering from outside the Cathedral, all clearly audible within, and by the end of it all the nation and much of the outside world had taken Diana, Princess of Wales to its heart. The drive back to Buckingham Palace and the triumphant appearances on the balcony—including the celebrated kiss which satisfied the crowd's clamour and probably set a precedent for the future—provided the evidence of the huge popularity which the Prince, during the previous decade, and the Princess, in only half a year, had established for themselves.

Diana's going away was no less enthusiastically watched: wearing a two-piece ensemble in soft cantaloupe pink, with a small, jaunty, feathered hat, she left the Palace by carriage with Prince Charles and was cheered all the way to Waterloo Station,

Record of a happy return to Balmoral: Charles and Diana, suntanned and in high spirits, at the Brig o' Dee on the Balmoral estate on

19th August, within a week of returning from their Mediterranean honeymoon.

and again from the station at Romsey, where they arrived two hours later, to Broadlands where they spent the first couple of days of their honeymoon. When, after a serenely peaceful break, they emerged again, it was only briefly that the British public saw them at Eastleigh airport as they left for Gibraltar. Five hours later they had arrived on the Rock where loyal and vociferous crowds, besieged for twelve years by the Spanish government's closure of Gibraltar's border with Spain, could not express their feelings sufficiently forcefully to their new

Princess in the short time it took for her and her husband to travel from Government House to the quayside.

For the stay in Gibraltar lasted only two hours before Charles and Diana were off on the Royal Yacht Britannia for a two-week honeymoon in the Greek islands. Their peace and isolation were unbroken and they spent their time swimming off private beaches, visiting archaeological sites, and generally enjoying being alone together during one of the hottest spells in Europe that summer. They completed this foreign part of the honeymoon with a visit to President Sadat of Egypt, upon whom Diana clearly made a good impression, judging by the affectionate way in which he embraced her at the end of their two-day acquaintance.

It was with mixed feelings that Diana left the Mediterranean for the cooler and breezier climes of Balmoral. She and Charles had certainly made the most of being away from it all and the end of their idyll must have seemed like a broken dream. At the same time, Diana confessed herself glad to be back at Balmoral —"the best place on earth," she called it. Looking back, it is probably easy to see why: the picnic on the day of Mountbatten's assassination, the first meaningful meeting with Charles, the rendezvous from Birkhall, a week-end soon after their engagement, a five-day break after Charles' return from tour in May— all took place at Balmoral, where Charles himself confesses his own affinity with his destiny and the history of his family.

If the rumours are to be believed, however, not all went well, and Diana's apparent inability to adapt to the domestic ways of her in-laws began to cause problems. Evidently, everyday life took on a formality she was unaccustomed to and thought unnecessary, and the long-drawn-out dinners and after-dinner conversations bored her. She could not get used to treating the servants in the royal manner—which was presumably too curt and peremptory for her own temperament to assimilate. But the biggest bone of contention was hunting: she was reported not to relish the constant outings to shoot grouse and deer, and it is even said that she refused the present of a gun-dog from the Queen on those grounds. Months later, a further rumour seemed to confirm her antipathy towards hunting when a tiff at Sandringham was reported to have occurred in which she told Charles sharply: "You know I didn't want to come here in the first place." Her dislike, if it exists, of blood sports may have been intensified by the furore caused by the undenied accusation that she had shot a stag whilst at Balmoral: this allegation was spiced with details of her bad aim, how the stag had to be finished off by other members of the party, and how she had attended the final grailloch—the disembowelling of the stag.

Unsavoury as these reports were, Diana appeared unaffected by them when she attended the Braemar Games for the first time early in September and on her subsequent occasional outings to London and Highgrove. These trips apart, the honeymoon—as one newspaper complained—"went on and on," until finally, at the end of October Charles took Diana to Wales to introduce her to the Welsh people for the first time as their Princess. The three-day tour was a success beyond all expectations. From the far north to the extreme south of the principality the couple were received by a sea of smiling faces, a forest of waving hands and the continuous deafening roar of welcoming voices. And it was, of course, Diana whom they came, in weather which was rarely clement and sometimes

abysmal, to see. She responded in true form, shaking hands with everyone, spending time to talk with the disabled, crouching down to listen to children, receiving heaps of bouquets, posies, single flowers and gifts of all kinds. The culmination of the whole visit was the almost emotional ceremony at the City Hall Cardiff, where Diana was honoured with the Freedom of the City.

my wife has had upon everybody."

That effect has, for those who hold the Royal Family dear, been immense. Both as the fiancée and as the wife of the Prince of Wales, Diana has delighted thousands of people with her very personal and warm approach to her duties. Adults have marvelled at the confidence of a young woman rocketed so suddenly from comparative obscurity to the position of third lady

A smiling face in a smiling crowd: (1) Diana is delighted with the colourful posy of flowers she received while in Hyde Park in November 1981; (2) a more sedate moment during her walkabout in *Builth Wells the previous month; (3) shaking hands with all and sundry while touring North Wales two days earlier.* Overleaf *Royal beauty: Diana in portraits taken by Snowdon in March 1981.*

in the land. Children have been thrilled that a person of royal rank should readily come amongst them and make them so important a part of her day. She has joined the Royal Family at a time when the younger generation is about to emerge, and she seems to be bridging the gap between the monarchy's middle-aged authority and the bevy of youngsters waiting in the wings. In doing so she focuses attention on the continuing process by which the duties of older members of the Royal Family are gradually handed over to the younger ones. In time, Diana herself will assume an increasing number of duties as the Queen narrows her field of engagements to encompass mainly those requiring her constitutional presence and involvement. If in taking on those heavier responsibilities Diana maintains the rate of progress which has made the past year such a success, that will be reason enough for her future subjects to say: "Well done; God Bless the Princess of Wales."

Only a few engagements followed that eventful tour before the news broke, taking everyone quite by surprise, that Diana was expecting a baby. Something close to astonishment at the speed of her pregnancy was exceeded only by the delight at the prospect of the birth of a direct heir to the Throne, and Buckingham Palace was again the magnet which drew the crowds on the morning of that crisp November day. Diana herself was lunching with Charles at the Guildhall, and heard both her husband and the Lord Mayor of London himself heap praises upon her for what Charles called "the wonderful effect

For weeks during the summer and early autumn *of 1980, Diana was pursued by photographers and reporters every time she left her Knightsbridge flat or the Pimlico kindergarten where she taught. These pictures show the difficulties she faced.*

Above *she walks to her car, ignoring the questions of her pursuers, but once inside, she cannot resist a peep before she drives off.* Opposite page *these pictures of Diana arriving at or leaving the now famous red door of the kindergarten building*

illustrate the tolerance and sense of humour which characterised most of her relations with the Press. She was frequently seen in the red Mini Metro car in which she is (bottom picture) about to drive away, but which she sold after her marriage.

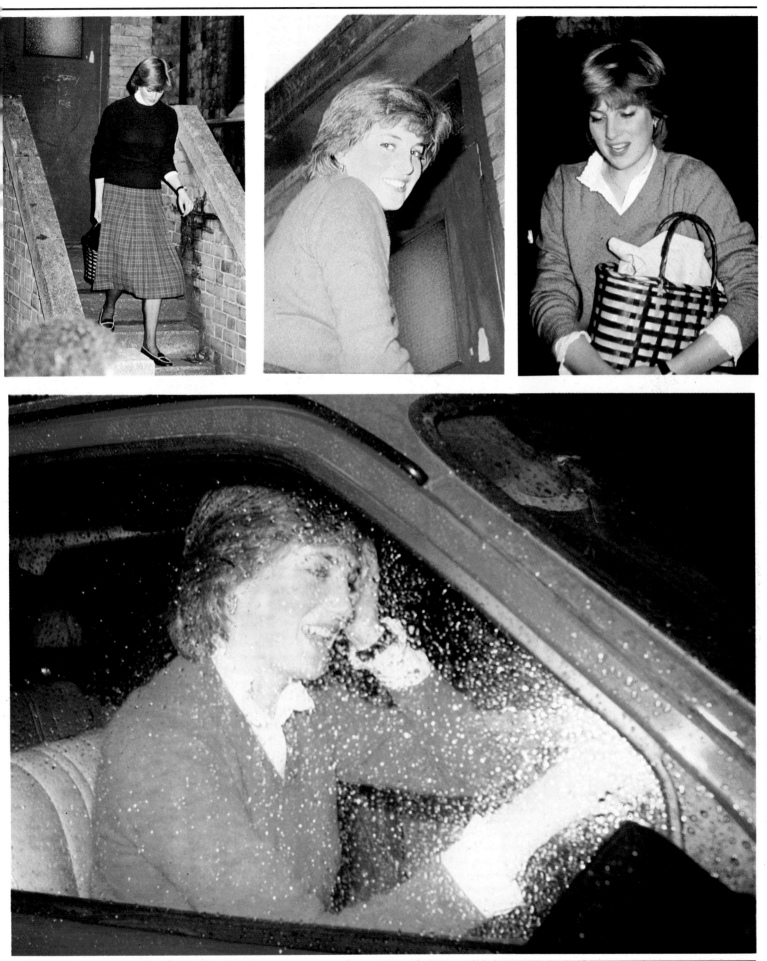

FIRST NIGHT OUT

On 9th March 1981 Charles and Diana attended a recital at Goldsmiths Hall in the City of London, held in aid of the Royal Opera House Development Appeal of which Charles is Patron. Normally the guest of honour—in this case Princess Grace of Monaco (seen, opposite, talking to Prince Charles at the reception) would have been the talking point, but it was the first official occasion on which Charles and Diana were in public together, and the crowds who gathered outside were hoping for their first glimpse of Diana herself. When she arrived (3) her revealing black dress stole the show and became instant headline news. The pictures below show Charles and Diana being escorted from the recital (2) and Diana sitting in the royal car (1) waiting to be driven back to Buckingham Palace. Overleaf more pictures of their arrival at Goldsmiths Hall and of the reception which preceded the recital.

1

2

3

FIRST NIGHT OUT

Previous page, *Lord Snowdon's delightful formal and informal portrait studies of Diana, taken in March 1981 and released for publication prior to her wedding. This page, Diana in animated mood (1, 2) at Cheltenham on 27th March 1981, where she visited the headquarters of the Gloucestershire Constabulary who now supervise the security arrangements for Highgrove. But the age of chivalry is not dead: schoolboy Nicholas Hardy offers Diana a daffodil (3) and then successfully aks if he might kiss the hand of his future Queen. Diana is obviously delighted with the gesture of homage and accepts it in the same spirit. Opposite page, Diana had everything to be pleased about: earlier that day the Privy Council had given its assent to her forthcoming marriage, which had by then been planned for 29th July.*

3

1

2

4

MOUNTBATTEN MEMORY

On 9th May, Diana spent a pleasant day with Charles visiting Broadlands, the eighteenth century mansion standing in 6,000-acres of parkland in the rich Hampshire countryside on the banks of the River Test. Charles opened an exhibition showing aspects of his great-uncle Lord Mountbatten's life of service to Britain, and the visit was commemorated by the planting of a sapling in the grounds. Charles was first to try his hand (4), and though Diana obviously did not think much of his witticisms, Lord and Lady Romsey, their hosts, enjoyed the humour of the occasion.

Eventually (2) Diana was persuaded to put in a couple of spadefuls and her job was done. Afterwards (1) she went round the perimeter of the enclosure to talk to some of the hundreds of people who came from Romsey and the surrounding district to be there. (3) Diana in her distinctive dress, at the end of the ceremony.

MEETING THE NEIGHBOURS

Highgrove, Charles and Diana's large country house, is one of three royal residences in Gloucestershire, and Tetbury is the nearest town. In May 1981 Charles and Diana spent a morning visiting the local hospital, where Charles opened a new operating theatre, and attended a thanksgiving service in the town's main church.

HIGH FASHION

6

7

Previous page, *Ascot, Windsor, Horse Guards Parade, the West End—Diana's fashion sense began to flourish and set trends. (1) Diana, wearing a cool dress, watches Charles playing polo at Windsor. (2) She accompanies Charles to the State Banquet given at Claridge's by King Khalid of Saudi-Arabia, and wears a light but full evening gown. (3) A splashy hat and flying veil for the Trooping the Colour ceremony. (4) Edwardian-style elegance at Ascot. (5) Attending the première of "For Your Eyes Only," the James Bond film, at the Odeon, Leicester Square. (6) Diana in candy stripes at Ascot. (7) Breezy fashion at St Margaret's Westminster where Charles was best man to Nicholas Soames.* This page, *Charles escorts Diana to the first day of Royal Ascot: (4) the royal carriage procession approaches the racecourse for the traditional parade. On the following two days, Charles was away in the United States, and Diana was accompanied by Princess Alexandra of Kent (1).* Overleaf, *the view across the Mall toward Carlton House Terrace as Diana approaches in the Glass Coach on her wedding day.*

3

WEDDING DAY

Diana, just discernible, waves to the appreciative crowds in the Mall on her way to St Paul's Cathedral. (3) With her father on the Cathedral steps. (4) The service underway: Diana stands next to Charles, both families looking on. (2) Leaving on Charles' arm.

Previous page, *the bride's ivory-coloured train*
makes a spectacular picture as she begins to climb
the Cathedral steps with her father. These pages,
the impressive bridal procession headed by the
Archbishop of Canterbury and other clergy,
progresses up the nave of St Paul's (4). After the
main part of the service, the Archbishop
pronounces his blessing on the newly-married
couple (3). During a brief pause, Charles finds
time to exchange a quick word with his new wife
(2). Eventually (1) the Archbishop leads Charles
and Diana to the high Altar where prayers are said
(5) to end the service. Overleaf, the Prince and
Princess progress down the nave, and all eyes
eagerly follow them.

MEETING THE PEOPLE

The greatest moment of all came as, to a massive, tumultuous and unending reception, Diana, on Charles' arm, reached the West Door of the Cathedral and came within sight of thousands of celebrating people (opposite). *For a few moments the couple paused to acknowledge the cheers (1) then they began the long walk down the* red-carpeted steps *(2) towards their waiting carriage — the 1902 State Postillion Landau. After a few seconds to settle in and adjust her intricate bouquet (3, 4) Diana and Charles were off on the triumphant journey back to Buckingham Palace. (5).* Overleaf, *Charles and Diana enjoying the ecstatic ovation from the crowds.* Following pages, *further stages in the homeward procession: a sea of smiling, shouting or merely curious faces, and a mass of flags and periscopes greet the royal couple as they travel through the London streets.*

ENCORE!

Previous page, *happiness shines in Diana's face as she waves in response to the crowd's exuberant good wishes (4).* Then, after the return to Buckingham Palace, it is time for the ever-popular balcony appearances *(3, 4)—and Charles gives Diana an appreciative kiss.* **This page,** *more scenes from the balcony—with pages Edward van Cutsem, and bridesmaids (bottom picture, left to right) Sarah Jane Gaselee, Catherine Cameron and Clementine Hambro.* Overleaf, *bride, groom, supporters, bridesmaids and pages—Patrick Lichfield's formal picture.* **Following pages,** *the families join in for the official photograph.*

HONEYMOON FORTNIGHT

Previous pages, *Family, guests and staff flock out of the Palace courtyard to wish Godspeed to the royal couple as they leave for their honeymoon, and a suited Charles, with Diana in a smart, soft pink outfit, wave to the cheering crowds at the Palace gates. Eyes and cameras record a last glimpse of them both as they are driven at the trot into the Mall on their way to Waterloo Station. They were a few minutes late leaving, but the honeymoon special—a locomotive appropriately named "Broadlands"—waited for them on Platform 12.* This page, *Charles and Diana wave (1) to the population of Gibraltar as, having arrived at the harbour, they leave the car which brought them from Government House. They turn round*

1

for a last look (2) before boarding the Royal Yacht Britannia for their two week honeymoon in the Mediterranean. Diana, happy to be on her way, acknowledges (3) the farewells of the people who came and waited to see her off. Overleaf, *(1) Diana in Egypt: about to take leave of President and Mme Sadat at the end of the royal couple's short stay. (2) Gibraltar's tribute to Charles and Diana makes it difficult for them to extricate themselves from their car at the dockside.* Following pages, *Charles and Diana on board Britannia—enjoying being alone together.*

2

1

2

1

2

3

4

This and following pages, *in mid-August Charles and Diana returned from Egypt to Balmoral where they were based until the end of October. On 19th August they took a stroll along the stony banks of the River Dee to be photographed for the first time since their return. Charles wore his Gordon Highlander kilt; Diana sported a thick, loose squared suit to keep out the cool Balmoral breeze.*

FUN AND GAMES

The Highland Games at Braemar are invariably watched by the Royal Family as one of the few public events of their long summer holiday in Scotland. Diana's first experience of them came in September when she accompanied Charles and his parents and brothers to watch the 1981 meeting. Appropriately she wore a chic plaid jacket and skirt and an eye-catching Tam o' Shanter beret. To complete the tribute to Scotland, she was presented with an ornamental spray of Highland heather.

A PRINCESS FOR WALES

Diana's first day in Wales took her to major towns in the North, from Deeside to Caernarvon. At the Deeside Leisure Centre she spent much of her time, predictably, with the youngsters (this page and overleaf); *whilst at Caernarvon she greeted the Constable, Lord Snowdon, with an affectionate kiss* (above).

BROWNIE'S HONOUR

On the second day of the royal tour of Wales, the weather broke with a vengeance but Diana gamely ignored the pouring rain, the rivers of rainwater which rushed down the streets, and the virtual destruction of her ostrich-feathered hat as she continued with her scheduled programme.

Diana and Charles visited St David's on their second day and attended a thanksgiving service at the Cathedral (left). Unfortunately part of the service was in Welsh and at times Diana felt it prudent to keep a low profile. Overleaf, at the end of that day Charles and Diana attended a gala concert at the Brangwen Hall,

Swansea: Diana received a bouquet (4) and Charles a miniature coronet (1)—presumably for the as yet unannounced new baby! At the end of the entire tour, they went to the City Hall, Cardiff (2) where Diana received the Freedom of the City.

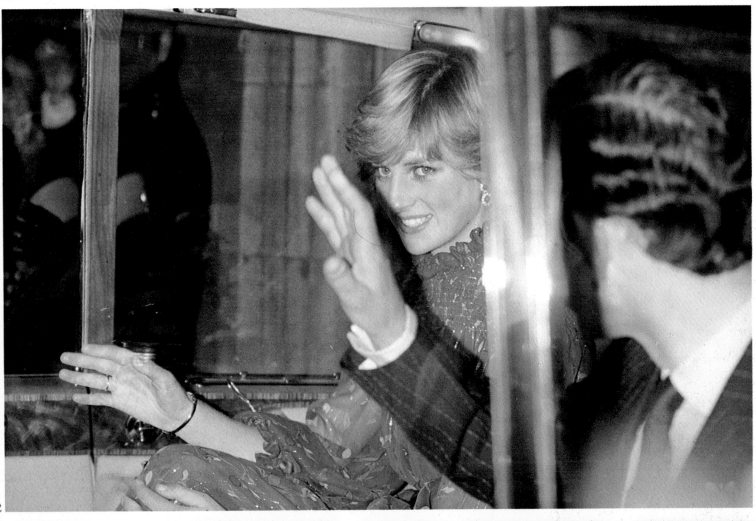

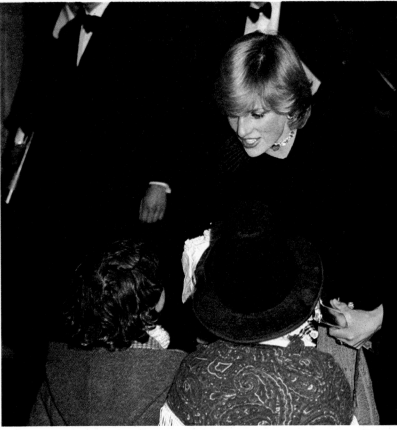

GREETINGS FROM SOUTH WALES

Previous pages, *bright-eyed Diana —
in London and Wales. Diana's
reception in South Wales was
rapturous. Her walkabouts were a
succession of conversations with
children from whom she received
more flowers than she could cope
with,* this page, *and meetings with
adults who braved threatening skies
to see their new Princess,* overleaf.

1

2

3

4

HAPPY ENDING

1

2

3

4

A BABY IS EXPECTED

Diana and Charles at the Guildhall, London, where they attended a luncheon given by the Lord Mayor, Sir Ronald Gardner-Thorpe (2). Diana arrived (3) full of smiles, since the news that she was expecting a baby had only two hours previously been announced. Sir Ronald referred in his speech of welcome to the news as the hallmark on the gold ingot of the royal wedding. (1) Diana leaving the Guildhall after the luncheon, to the cheers of wellwishers outside. (4) Diana's first solo engagement—switching on the Christmas lights in Regent Street, London in December. She had by then overcome the morning sickness which had forced her to cancel many previous engagements.

1

2

3

CELEBRATING CHRISTMAS

On 21st December, Charles and Diana went to Guildford Cathedral where local schools and organisations put on a special Christmas celebration in aid of the Prince's Trust — one of several charities with which Prince Charles is directly concerned, and which seeks to help disadvantaged children and young people in their efforts to improve their own environment. Wearing yet another bright, stunning outfit, Diana quickly made herself at home, and was soon in the midst of the children who acted out the Nativity scenes (2, 3, 5). The pictures overleaf shows her in the happiest of moods, thoroughly enjoying her evening out.

3

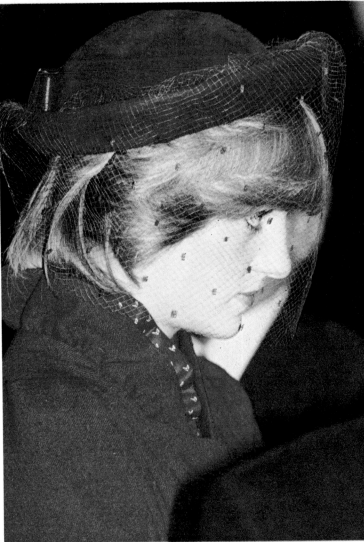

4

5

A CAKE TO CUT

A surprise item, not on the agenda, was the Christmas cake which the Trust suddenly produced, and which Charles and Diana were asked to cut (2, 4). With their wedding only five months behind them it was fairly obvious what they were thinking about as they obliged! (3) Charles and Diana leaving the Cathedral after the service, and walking out into the snow which had

1

2

not discouraged hundreds of people from waiting outside throughout the service for the chance to see them both again.

3

NEW YEAR VISIT

Between Christmas and February, Diana was seen only rarely in public. On Christmas Day she joined the rest of the Royal Family for Morning Service at St George's Chapel Windsor, and accompanied the Queen and her immediate family to Sandringham for the New Year Holiday. There were occasional sightings of her at Sandringham church, but her first official appearance after Christmas was at the Dick Sheppard School at Tulse Hill in South East London, where she and Charles attended the January Fair. As always on such occasions she was in good form—buying the occasional item from the stalls, being presented with toys—including a huge teddy-bear for her baby—and even winning on the Tombola stall. Overleaf, one of the dangers of meeting your public is illustrated as this toddler reaches out and pulls at one of Diana's coat buttons (2). But it is all part of a day's work, and Diana's charming smile (1) as she leaves the school suggests that she has thoroughly enjoyed it all.

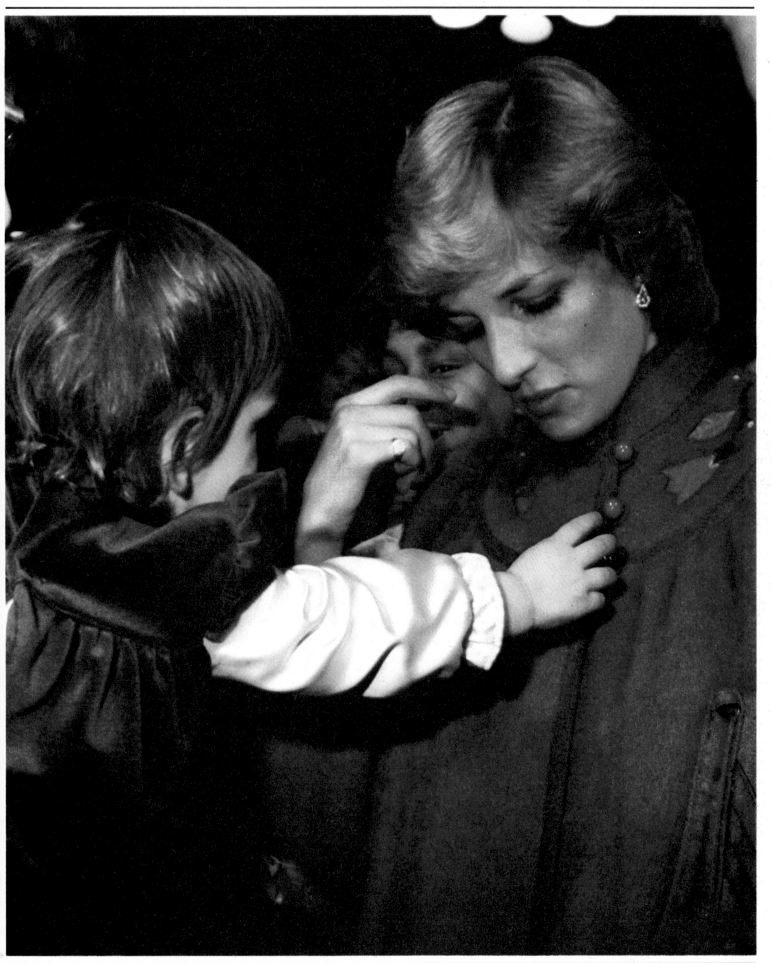

PRINCESS OF HEARTS

Diana's visit with Charles to Tulse Hill was her first to South London since her marriage, and was undertaken to support a fund raising campaign to send pupils of the Dick Sheppard school on an educational visit to Zimbabwe, whose independence celebrations Charles had attended in 1980. It was clearly a popular decision with the children of this multi-ethnic school who played host to their royal visitors in the informal way that always brings out the best in Diana.

Since that occasion, her official duties have been few and far between, and in mid-February she and Charles went to the island of Eleuthera for a ten-day holiday, staying at Windermere, a property owned by the Mountbatten family. After Easter, Diana will not carry out any further engagements, as she prepares for the birth of her first child in June. The baby will be the first direct heir to be born to a Princess of Wales since 1864, and will be second in line of succession. Diana will thus become the mother of a prospective king or queen of the United Kingdom, and a new chapter in her life will begin.

Designed by Philip Clucas MSIAD
Produced by Ted Smart and David Gibbon

GOD BLESS THE PRINCESS OF WALES

A CORGI BOOK   0 552 99008 6

First publication in Great Britain

PRINTING HISTORY

Corgi edition published 1982
Copyright © 1982 Colour Library International Ltd.,
    New Malden, Surrey, England.
Colour separations by FER-CROM, Barcelona, Spain.
Display and text filmsetting by Focus Photoset,
    London, England.
Printed and bound in Italy by A. Mondadori - Verona
All rights reserved.

Corgi Books are published by Transworld Publishers Ltd.,
Century House, 61-63 Uxbridge Road, Ealing, London W5 5SA.